Private Lemonade

John Godfrey

ADVENTURES IN POETRY

Printed in Canada
Book Design by *typeslowly*

Some of these poems appeared in *Sal Mimeo* and *Shiny*.

Cover design taken from *Egyptian Ornament* by P. Foøtova-Šámalová,
(Allan Wingate/ London), Copyright © 1963 by ARTIA

Adventures in Poetry titles are distributed through *Zephyr Press* by
Consortium Book Sales and Distribution [www.cbsd.com] and by
SPD: Small Press Distribution [www.spdbooks.org].

ISBN 0-9706250-70-4

9 8 7 6 5 4 3 2 FIRST PRINTING IN 2003

ADVENTURES IN POETRY

NEW YORK   BOSTON

WWW.ADVENTURESINPOETRY.COM

Contents

Everything Beautiful

Buick, big old boat, purrs
Backs into the square of moonlight
where the path is worn

Notice you must the pang
in the air
        You hear
a little of bells, a little of hypnosis

I have traced all this to my body
Everything beautiful, and everything
that ever goes wrong

One giant light of green
and one of gold, inject the glow
chosen sky by the city

Vogue

Growth flavor air
Even the evening
     dully illumines
Everything tires
     the dew
blown dirt
Heads turn
     consensual royalty
Brown cheek
     bleached elbow
Desire present
     Longing not yet
          accented by bedrooms
Dirty blue light
smoked with dust
Under it parked cars
all appear expensive
Elegance continues
her way, leaves
     on my sleeve
a rank

Shadow Feet

Sweetheart   debt   blue heels
The dominant hand
of my partner
            at 4 o'clock
on the power steering

The little bit of time
you have, knowing

I had better wait here
for the canned laugh
Shadows joined at
the feet
            smoothly
smoothly tread

Plush You

Some
      sunset
            thing

Cocktail
      fill
            moves

Three
      mind
            love

Banquette
      plush
            you

Down
      it
            comes

After
      all—
            lips

Disbelief

Usage
        clouded and fast
                Gyrotrophic

Eye out for
      her
            least
                    expression
Hissing of leaves

As words go
        meditation
            is small
She apprehends

This window
        for diminuendo
            forecast

She looks abstractedly
        at the fender
            pull away

Unnameable

You come in cold draft
        taste me, leave
                nothing behind

Invisibility
        lends you surprise
                and mortality

To feel your fingers
        cold on my ears
                The call of blackout

Shortcuts

Nobody knows shortcuts
Endure amounts of time

Comes out during the race
Makes speech sound lovely

Refer to it at the cave
See wonders of gambling

I say try me sometime
The rest soon contends

Far away I remember
My call where I wander off

Put on shoes and talk
Follow deep in the ground

Gravy

Gravy is important
      Patois excitement
            Totally unrecognizable

Long for hot nights
      Bus color sky
            Hands on wheel

Sporting chap gone silver
      Queue up for hire
            Identity dialect

Door slams wet guy's smoke
      Own people call you boy
            Idiot light goes on

Battery

Private Lemonade

Some days I forget
    In my own home
        high stakes charades

And spouts pour copiously
    on every sensorium
        to flood the hobo camp

He answered to Friar
    Himself a wandering few steps
        in two trips around the basement

Melody is more than a name
    An obbligato in front of the stride
        I saw him peel his own ivories

It goes in one ear and stays put
    This exacting moment
        Undetectable difference

Footprints

Rings float in night
They return to big hands

Pigeon ruff flutters in gust
Wet footprints bear resemblance

Cheap blue tumbler in daylight
After I tie his shoes

My windows all infected
A vast country but audible

I mean "blizzard" figuratively
Dust spares narratrix

Talk is cheap move on
Separate and cool

That Place Anymore

To be learned
     from but not
          to believe

Influence
     surroundings
          demonically

Even your
     sarcasm shows
          you loyal

Twelve strings
     Sympathetic
          yellow jello

Your hand brush
     ashes from
          my eyebrows

That is just
     horrible
          Have a seat

Dents

You were never this
      beautiful light at night
            I can only hear

Of all that abides
      Small influences
            There's temperature

for instance, beside you
      Like many car dents
            Snow corrects it all

I could tell you things
      Fantastic longtime
            You aren't the first

Rockin'

Blue wrapped in gray
Leaves underfoot orange
Intensely sweet mold
A gift

It should be one of us
Source of meagre light
Just because I move
      Autumn winter autumn
      Frame and shoot

Weeping too unusual
Fatigue an indication
      Change unnoticed

Check for bruises
Say open your eyes
Squalid but fruitful
      Cease to exist

Rockin' back and forth

Find Out

Nothing at all behind it
        Pointed out in crowds or
                stunted and ballsy

They have only that one place
        You find out how to be one
                Something glad and slick

Meteoric sand for jewelry
        Try to sing of chopped hair
                You squirm and deliver cues

Replace the stone with water
        Not at all solid mono blue
                I could fault the poison

Possible to kill and stick around
        Anger expressed as clothing
                Needlers mounted on cinderblocks

Infidel affection dogs the crosswalk
        Thirst, arrest, and confetti
                Only a careless spell

Idiot Might

Reserved for the bevy
Lighter light, colder
fatal secrets, lies told
more children at work

Discovered during fits
of construction: formula
for return to powder
At the end, mate dust

They look me in the eye
Try as an idiot might
I cannot defend minds
I want to see, I'll pay

Take comfort in a crowd
windblown waiting for cabs
To claim to be funny
To stand up in the tub

Give Off

Thoughts stolen
        Sun cave dwells
                Stumblebum

Don't hesitate
        Pretty goodlooking
                Different world

Tonight's a start
        You must be
                to be with you

Out of nowhere
        Chopper dopplers o'er
                Your tobacco stains

Comfort at right times
        Cooler immersion
                Swimming in dimes

You give off wisps
        Letter by letter
                All the questions

Bleach

This winterless Spring
Equinoctial bleach in highlights
In thrall occurs a lapse

Your voice over traffic
Never less symphonic
Waited and waited

Print of rattan on your calf
Succinct and nearly cruel
Turns lamplight lavender

I am gone
You are gone
Let it now begin

Anywhere

Foolish bright nowhere thing
Hand open through bars
Wind rattles over crap

Penlight searches for map
There is one token left
Dull crease of moonlight

Conservation of error
Brokenhearted boy you hated
Dry sheet too a mistake

A girl can stand like that
Lights on wheels strobe
Palms drip on shoes

Vitals

Imperfect hand
Unrepresentative
large square forehead

They are on fire
You must choose
body piercings

Shoeful of wild
children, agonists
of venality

Moldering cold
The requisite
impervious clothes

Frozen breathings
Sufficient rockets
Parallel arms

Shiny litter
You squint downtown
Forgot your gloves

Downy Skin

Compared to
my life
my life
is long

Accomplish
a tenuous
fixation
Memory

Anything
anyone
can, will, or fails
to intimate

It is older
I knew it
long ago
Downy skin

Jubilee

Sidewalk of your street
in my dessert
      Boycott
on the automatic pillow

Many claims to thought
So many pierced tongues
      Transreaction
I leave before I wonder

There should be an ordinal
and some valves
      Stranger
and in every way a mountain

One more ride necessary
Coordination loan to queen
      Details
less all credits to sensorium

And so the heath as a scalp
A woman of valor
      Surprises
Leaks in the oddest places

Phenomenal

Density of heavens
Ephemeral attrition
Curls of smoke
from telephone corner

Hello miss pert
in tight lime skin-thins
I imagine that
the world has not stopped

Drawing water, Lulu?
Air so thick and nutty
women overscent themselves
Naked skin in relief

The Beautiful One

Like a flower bending
from momentum of light
        Anotherness
Placid as a lead snake

Knowing from inside out
Cause, in effect, a search
        I love you like
the mountain loves sand

Spread ground on the hand
Dawn and day slightly coincide
        Remember me
Force you to listen

Something Up

My man Jackson
     Call the peanut
         trays away

Moon takes out
     sky with needles
         Falls in dust

The stink sweetens
     I hope it's an
         ass I see curve

Making something
     up realistically
         You dare to spill

Personal as time awaits
     Blunt blows rain
         from opposing thumbs

Soothe

The inside of my thigh
slides down from
the sun
through ceilings

I lift you
in front of me
        so you bend over my hair
            I exhaust you
      by listening

I soothe by getting small
There's no greater
          distance
      than from you to
         night

Express

If I wanted to
      say look out
            a windshield

The way you talk
      Toy with radio
            Roll window down

Smoke carries your breath
      No mirror that sees
         you in it

Spread

Kleenex and money
      Keys to dangle
            Modest panties

Twice for starters
      Narrower alley
            Warrants situation

Dirty hair perfect
      Chew chenille spread
            Wrong shoes for dust

Light hovering in snow
      Legs crease percale
            Walking equals sleep

Strokes

The rabble I commit
      The rubble rather I rob
            Wheels touch and go

So I wolf down my clams
      Heathen heels stake the body
          Tapestry tunes

Cheek smooth from jaw to piercing
      Fingerprint fog cools to nil
          She paints the tub

If awake you're twice alone
      Breath dark not the room
          Big baby loon

Front Seat

Seventy-eight ripples
        Forty-five shakes
Light warped on dull
        uniform Ike eros
No need to worry
        The man don't love you
An item of undercloth
        The uninterupted front seat
Everybody singing
        Merry Christmas and inside
It seems one hundred
        years of Christmas war
And if I want to
        love that woman
Always end on a chord
        Suffer in vain

Knowhow

Never quite habiliments
See-through trees
Eyes floored by leaves

Your name comes back
Everything heated
Dress for the cold

No one forgets
Assemblage aflame
in store windows

A very long letter
First time time succeeded
So many bus rides

High degree farewell
Later much later
What not to feel

Pool Cake

When she sleeps on the floor
When the umbrella blows
into her hand

The whole landslide is missing
She treats me like a conversion
I am a probability

Eclipses her in sheets of snow
How many emotions on
the tines of a fork

Her particular disguise for dust
The haves are equidistant in time
You could say everything is minus that

To those who waken stealthily
Sew up the hat real neat
Frost ascends the blade

It

You you you *what?*
How you do without?

Curves end in curves
Not me she's after

Shed without walls
Eventually femme loses

And it is so small
Change

Blush

The land is
squashed
      between
gases and bones

Petals of apple
      Animated buzzing
Your forearms
        blush

Never forget that
I learned from
        wonder
    Proportions
appeared to me

Rain sounds the roof
    softly
     too, on leaves
And then there was one

Can't Say

Can't say I don't
      Fire hazard or mouthwash
            Mud on the gizmo

Grimy handed
      Baby dimples
            Hair like breeze

Terrified
      Object was never
            before without say

World sways around
      Other farce renews
            Short bridge to sell

Flourish

Midnight shower
  Baby blue feet
    Forget the cigarette

Petition own power
  Plant a cleat
    Which bachelorette

Turned fine as flour
  Thought twice to meet
    Eye on folded net

Unlit stairs at any hour
  Hips wise to seat
    Out-of-breath wet

Eye fatigue narrows
  Burns chartreuse with conceit
    Frozen *tête-à-tête*

Flood Monkey

The spider on flagstaff
   Translucent gray cloth
      Clocktower blurs

Teen chest warm spells
   from open black vests
      Grit touched with fragrance

I chill at the might
   Flatlands invent ringed fingers
      Bed marinates in whatever

Imagine my caresses
   I hold on to objects that float
      My eyes repair to you

I call up her lights
   She neatly folds it
      Air arrives from anywhere

Dim, Dud

Dim realism, dud parquetry
pried off sidewalk
Commonality in due course

A hand no longer cold
Illusory violet branch tip
The girl looks ever younger

Vitiated serene kids
Reflections off my reflections
The scale played this evening

Trousers cling by down draft
Directions balance at zero
My own resonant footsteps

Everyday begins the same
I sleep whenever possible
Large indifferent appetite

Weathered ill cared for hands
I am tired yet ready
The helpless reappear

Protection

When I go
    out I don't
        fall asleep

Children will
    be always
        on target

Cold bites deep
    into mixed
        company

Houses fall
    that have once
        already

Protection
    remains how
        unlikely

I am glad
    You begin
        to worry

You'll survive
    You'll forget
        Shiftless luck

Dream Marble

Midnight shines like sun
Her language rhymes laugh with cough
Her continent produces "shooting fog"
I witness a dead planet glow
through a glassless window
in the elevator

Pockets develop among hills and bays
where the world is small and
always smells the same as
her home
       I go to it
but in fact it is here
I have always had here with me here
My first impression was of
dream marble statues and led
me to perceive that this city

in honorable, selfish ways
emits into the air I breathe
the power and felicity of pronouns

Rain

Perfect ten it seems
    Mortar fires in drums
Sense of a meal
    where was none

Hair combed the secret
    Boor now knight
How poor how foreign
    Gone where is she

Confound the donor
    Catastrophic diversion
The other side of bloodlines
    are borders

I find you at length
    Always know I search
The veil comes down
    Print of your boot

In mud my consolation

Three Ways

Introduce silence
Lamplight close to
     one gilded foot

Featureless sky, retro bells
Noon, fantasy dulls
     Confident you will
         be understood
Let no one overlook
the sanitary angle
Smoke enters the light

Change divided three ways
     Your kindnesses relent
I only recall so

You, maybe not, pause
Not I who
     opens the door
     It takes just a moment
for you never to have known

Shrewd Breed

Mañana banana
You crazy like boca sola
Spin man keep airtight
sequence please interfere

Departed all to pieces
Slow roll walk
Predator spotlight
from guy pants
Township without halls
Hide among friends
Don't see them at all

So it's warm and soft
and reaches to the sky
Tobacco flakes mixed with
radiant channels the end
impenetrably reconciled

Expect

It's only wind
    Strings of light
        Face all angles

What a bargain
    Not up to me
        Sweat under sweater

I remember what
    was at what location
        Ride's smoother now

I wait for you
    You contemplate
        how new you are

Amount

Something outside
amounts to everything
Air sped by
friction over
baggage and shirts
lifts both my hands
Casualties forgot
at the callbox
Legs simply everywhere
I have a lot
of what's more
You prefer to bare
your throat but
a victim is
not like you

Attrition

In moments of bloodlessness
There is really no use

When safety and falseness
share encomium

To seek recklessness
from an athletic clown

Everything that ever dies
is underwear to me

But from next Saturday
what is played like what

Rotation

Tree just might be
younger than you think
Smell weeps in hair

Sarod through window
Turn rather than step
Mutants on wheels

Push through the crowd
Liner shrinks your lips
Were you a star

Both of you please
Dust settles on car
The wait's over

Flakes

Muddy plastic spoon
Barefoot on colas
First they nab the tramp

Words sort and sink
Ash glitters on her collar
Jumpseat vapor smell

She interrupts herself
I too blow smoke
Can't hardly overhear

Farewells then walk alone
Night briefly unwraps
Inevitable hallways

Privacy

One two hundred
They are slick
They are slaves

Someone must be
Something done
Qualified laughter

Separate light
Everything quiets
You forget sleep

It is piracy
My hips on yours
No longer simpler

for everyone

Dusty Hands

Failure the intimate
name for darling
Dusty hands in
a cool room
I enter a heated one
When you get a chance

Only the smoke sets us apart
Holiday lights reflect you
on windowglass
                              at bar's end
Quite a hullaballoo
Goodnight, Mona
Your service was kind
Conversation quits, half a bottle
quickly order back
Pull coat close

Plunder

Charcoal highlight dubiety
So many hands pressing
cause the miracle to blanch

Produces tea from between
her legs when radio fades
Curriculum vitae debris

A grain of something pearly yellow
Crack like a smile in the wall
The iffy way you dress

The French Girl

Discomfitted
    Trailer girl
        Pantyhose

Shame driven
    Blotchy cheeks
        One skirt's all

Work gets her
    out where you
        assemble

Endlessly
    pouring down
        on her pride

Suspicious
    forever
        She attracts

Will she or
    not preclude
        affinity?

Carries her
    weight in grips
        of metal

Breaks down knee
    in cold mud
        face buried

Service
    in the sky
        Free regret

Worthy

She has one for *you*
      Fiery glow through alabaster
            You don't notice the bait

Impulse toddles in search
      Smell of wash over the phone
            Downstream always the thought

River smoothes wall of abyss
      Of the beginning a word
            As abundant as dimes

Handles glow with daybreak
      Wet wadded covers
            Inside a curtain of thighs

Dump

My name
　　　have been
　　　　　　scathe

Tender reaction
　　　Your footsteps
　　　　　　Call me hon

Achieve
　　　expensive
　　　　　　vocals

Hail cab, close
　　　Transported
　　　　　　Be easier

Dumped out
　　　of bedding
　　　　　　Curtains!

Water Everywhere

If it please your honor
    The heart is drug
        The hair is too new

Whispers on the sidewalk
    Glare in line of sight
        No particular woman

Shadow short and fat
    Refuse red car blue car
        Princess not at home

Like an idiot I do
    Clothing you can hear
        Smoke from potted palm

Mixed-up Supine

Mixed-up
  Supine
Sand in your dollars
   Broken panties
The one more casual
  Guided man

There has to be
  a surface
The other half
  is glands
Beholden to
  utter sleaze

I try to pin
  your wrists
the way
  you want
Get yourself
  your own rain
Now you're happy
  Frank blood

Big Picture

Daylight dies ("fades")
Blood strays to my penis
The promise was made
on another planet's couch

You get the photocopy
A profile recognizable halfway
down the elevator shaft
No drapes aflutter
Across the way observe
half a bodily action
Each star a naked window

Allons

A lot of toleration
It's funny that way
Door shuts, engine starts

Sky divides into
different whites
There is no room

And then catch you
Your skirt collapses
over my heels

I thought all that skin
meant a shape to trust
Between her and echoes

Pretend that time
is going forward
Explain white leaves

Cheer

They blow up
      Their creations
            harp in night air

The dead calculate
      Child chances miasma
            Smaller flags

Found in a drum
      Walk me down
            Directional bad

Dehiscence ends drought
      People age dry
            Big fat showoff

Baby Proofs

Special
       baby town
Overlook
       the hindrances
You and
       your proofs

Natural
       smiling boy
This is
       his grave
I told you
       — special

Attractions

Who'll be with me
    when wind sweeps
        through the museum

Why that hair not
    my color comes to rest
        on some of my own

Look down the doppler gun
    You're always playing
        and food goes to waste

The leader scurries special
    The ladder sways
        Profess aloud soon

at a theater near you

Filled Turn

Why they were tried
Booting on the corner
This and sub-that going on

The world breeze switches sets
Most go to the place of some
Unsteady table inside a railing

I have reamed I have reticulations
And still the stars do not matter
I partially bear my weight

I take in my hands
colorful bits of rug
Blood inherited by vectors

Comes a fragment of thrill
The azure is shatterproof
To repose in mild powers

Before You

There before you
        Onus of beauty
                Reflect gold floors

Pay the fare
        Light among girders
                in fact errs

One afternoon
        As ever prepared
                I captivate little

Noble the word
        So many intincts
                Take it away

Be There

Clerestory
       stomping grounds
Hand over mouth
       picaresque
You had to be there
       there and there

Vividness for granted
       Eye with a clue
Tropical brightness
       bred nostalgia
I was a right
       smart of heave-ho

Wings were broad
       Updraft was warm
Of course I might
       have not risen

Fuel Kiss

As long as I
can get my head
to fit the ground

The clown talks a lot
like Lee Marvin cranked
Somewhere, brokered silence

Now you discover
cleverness, you stretch
and dry some skins

This is my start
and this is my
discovery of registration

Papers, that's what
I lost my papers

Food of Others

Consideration
      for my sleep
            Bird of night

And by day
      getting used to
            the food of others

To be consistent
      with unkempt hair
            Fluff on fingertips

Your cheek is cool
      Your core is hot
            Song of your weight

Napkin

Gravity curls
Shoulders melt
into vapor
Broad body
of impure water
cures the sidewalk
Same door in as out
Little girl fun
aspires to wait
Thin doodle haze
Vast quantity of
crumbs yet no filet
Odor of andro smoke
would suit traffickers
Napkin no longer
worthy to dab blood
Lately it hasn't
been the same old
gravelly voice
I put my hand where
I better carry
sound like water

Parade

Inadvertent jitters
Everyone knows this street
Point of view all over again

Hat on it
Clipped heels bobbed tail
Then you know real rancor

Ghost in mother's milk
Heal worry heal weakness
Find private ocean

Voice loud love strange

People

As if peopled
      without an ear
            Much is made

Autumn leaves
      me nothing
            Emptier

A grace note
      An appliqué
            Subtle cure

Slope

I cannot say
    handbag for you
        Armrest's so cold

I do say it was
    all in weak minds
        Highway post mortem

On the drums I
    might black out
        The sleep of your foot

is vortex and yourself
    is wanton goof
        Where is everything

Known to you

Then the Brain

Then the brain
        one half mine
                Can't place it

Will you be
        Seventh Ring
                material

Will you shoot
        aloha scene
                at midnight

Exchange sky
        Study games
                Musical

Whole

I am lost and distracted
You have all the right ideas
I try to be whole

Abandonment
Stench eyesore
Whose bidding

You relative
I correlative
Debris all kinds

Be there sanctions
bearer wizens
Play by head

Back comes first
The moment comes forth
Handling of water

Bereftness once sweet
Singly together past
that beauty occasion

See you some
Albatross sensations
More always more

Sayonara

Let me take
    advantage
        of your wind

Some need ice
    So tiny yet
        you choose right

Otherwise
    sleeping bags
        City burns

Hunted by
    microbial
        entertainers

You have the gist
    It piles up
        Horizon

Importance

I enter leaking choices
> It is paint and phantasm
>> So much for naked fingers

Kinda walk is that?
> Conspicuous coat
>> I see your face on it

That blur is stairs
> Your legs gooseflesh
>> No one actually sees

Car handles familiar
> Fingernail taps window
>> Wordless your own reflection

Alight

The last thing I say
      Happen to be there
           You wouldn't know

Has to do with skirts
      Theater dark and all
           Our quarters on the seat

There is still time left
      Towers extinguish
           The sky's alright

Orange peel in your hair
      Perfume walks on forever
           This pillow only years

Priceless Sport

Coating of muddy dust
                    over time
            past the femme
the fatale

You reach
            with your cheek
                    for snowflakes

Skyline beacons in fuzz
                    I do not
            say of my mood
this priceless sport

You appeal to my hunger
            I study your shadows
Your right hand holds
            down its left
The door opens and
            shuts far away
The smoke moves

Original

I'm a year behind
the amount of
                    contraband
You have the donor code
                    Hid inside walls
She glows, refreshed

Instruments each with
                    its stick
The cloth folds gently
over seated thigh
There is the signal
                    for evening
                    up to begin

Poem

Nasty gust
    I bounce off
        renegades

Waiting for
    the true side
        of fragile

Ordinaire
    I open
        your left hand

See the burn
    Hear the ice
        under tires

Violated
    persons glow
        Windows close

You undress
    Alone I
        greet this thought

There's no end
       Remember
              the first, first

caught your eye
       In return
              smoke allowed

Equals

They never say it will
      Rose complected or not

Massive smokes push high
      The girl does it anyway

Sky doesn't lower twice
      Uses of air cease

I fly in fits and starts
      higher than tall buildings

Shorten my shrift
      Expunge the retinal soup

Without cunning, with posture
      Let alone a fallow lie

Injury

This is the street to do it
Make believe letters in my hand
If one is undeserving
of historical practices

Follow the pith helmet
Heather color of sand
and assassination both right
She more beautiful than horizon

Stress of shared helplessness
Don't mind please I'm inured
Call yourself bloated by Venus
Nothing but wet camisole

Why you can't stand up this time
Defects of light on black sky
Abandon the tongues of many
Delete description of moonlight

Tide

River with two straws
Light fails the moths
One cannot almost
touch Brooklyn
Dust stills in air
You try the door
Voices stop abruptly
Bridge lights in hair
Party of the first
part can't remember
Window opens slowly
I count three six nine

Heavy Building

Heavy as a doll
Prove to me I
have come full oval
The red phone I
answer it's
mongrels left to
pick up rocks

Left foot more sure
I don't notice
the cigarette until
my fingers are afire
The lighted arms
The mellowing time
The vanishing building
I swear it was there
and I once entered

Savor

Minutes pass descriptive smoke
Analgesia searches slaves
Conformations of your waist
instruct me in my hands
You make claims of the earth
yet are spared, being ridiculous

Walking pace river flows
Its sunlit tangled grays
My hands are sensitive weights
Left on your flank, right
on opposing current
I want to be certain
the betrayal of my
excitement has savor
Details in your hair

What

Lousy
You?
'Sa shame

Lostya
Hadya
Orderly

Freedom
Paltry
Sandwich

Have to
Maybe
Oopsy

Get out
No way
You through?

Wavy

Boogaloo
the best you can-can
Time hangs in braids

There is room for
that hip in the
blazing gold drum

Do not hasten
The crosswalk aglow
Maybe learn nothing

Signature footsteps
I know what to do
with the wrong dream

Creed

Belief in warning light
The leaves you part
Voice supposedly childlike

Result of vintage drizzle
Nipples and matted strands
Wet pavement's earthy spell

Seen on yonder stairs
Soiled fragrant hands
Truly open shoes

Newborn all in order
Air refluxes close
Admire mother's body

Can't take the rules

Known

He gives you waves of wares
    Had I known
        The stain of spilled something

And of course I hear them
    Sufficient monotony
        Day so mild it's not there

Questions only augment
    The tunnel dissolves
        One hand in the other

Dream More

It is dream more
of the day
than empty bed

I carry how
many empty
buckets?

We were meant
for each other
as new animals

Severally means
me, you, the other feet
I am ashamed

that when I
sleep your time
stands still

Never Lands

The heavy
    The bright

Marvelous bird
    Poison thermals

I call distances
    Stone never lands

Those are extra
    My heart warms

Overlooked Nomads

Complaint set to
music, chantoozie
stands on my feet

Overlooked when
leaving, full glass
drains into air

You are one clue
when you are your own
The wires burn up

Remain away
You nearly die
day after day

greater than I

Flash

Angles are discovered
You get the light right
    The floor
dematerializes

Yours is not
the only face

Air dries
Now we are
really cool